Lost In the Woods

By Grace Shevlin

Copyright © 2018 Face Shevlin

DEDICATION

To Mommy & Daddy, Charlotte & Caroline.

Lost In The Woods
By Grace Shevlin

Hi! My name is Melody. I have a dog named Spot and a friend named Sunny! I live at 15 Elmit Lane and I am 9 years old. Also, I have 2 older sisters and 2 younger brother and a baby sister!

Hi! My name is Sunny and I have a dog named Midnight and a friend named Melody. I live at 77 Mywin Rd. I have 2 older sisters, 2 older brothers and 2 younger sisters. They're twins!

"Let's go for a walk into the woods to find the waterfalls," shouted Sunny. "Okay! That sounds like a great idea. Let's go..." So they all set off down the street. Absolutely no cars or people were there. They crossed the quiet street and walked into the woods.

The woods were empty. "Come on Midnight. Come on Spot!" They called to their dogs. It was kind of spooky.

As they walked farther into the woods, more and more paths appeared. "Are you sure you know your way?" Melody asked feeling spooked.
"We"re fine. Just follow me." So they kept walking deeper into the woods

They didn't mind the paths. In fact, they didn't even notice them after a while. They were talking so much that they weren't paying any attention to each other. They were lucky to be staying close together. But that was all about to change.

"Hey, Melody! Are you sure we're not lost?" There was no answer. "Melody? Melody, where are you?" Sunny yelled at the top of her lungs.
"I AM LOST!"

"Ruff, Ruff" Midnight barked. " Oh no, Oh no, Oh no! Ssssh Midnight. I'm lost and I don't know what to do!" Midnight pulled and pulled on his leash so hard that Sunny let go and Midnight ran away!
"Oh no, Midnight!" She yelled after him.

Sunny followed Midnight as fast as her legs could carry her! " Midnight! Midnight! Come back here. MIDNIGHT!" Sunny called out. But Midnight didn't come back, he had a plan. Sunny called and called and if she didn't stop soon, she was going to loose her voice.

Finally she decided to follow Midnight. She ran and ran and finally Midnight stopped. She managed to catch up and realized Midnight was sniffing the air. But why?

She followed Midnight and heard a familiar voice. It was Melody!
" Melody, walk towards my voice!" Sunny started to yell again. Melody stayed calm and listened. She eventually found Sunny and together they began to walk. A few minutes later they saw a beautiful sight. The waterfalls! They sat down to look, talk and eat. When it was time to go home, they decided to hold hands and be extremely careful. They made a promise - not to get lost EVER again!

THE END

81691954R00018

Made in the USA
Lexington, KY
19 February 2018